D0989964

Green Cars:
Earth-friendly Electric Vehicles

John Coughlan

Capstone Press

MINNEAPOLIS

Printed in the United States of America.

Capstone Press • 2440 Fernbrook Lane • Minneapolis, MN 55447

Editorial Director   John Coughlan
Managing Editor   John Martin
Copy Editor   Theresa Early
Editorial Assistant   Michelle Wood

Library of Congress Cataloging-in-Publication Data

Coughlan, John.
    Green cars: earth-friendly electric vehicles / John Coughlan.
        p. cm.-- (Wheels)
    Includes bibliographical references and index.
    ISBN 1-56065-211-X (lib. bdg.)
    1. Electric vehicles--Juvenile literature. [1. Electric vehicles. 2. Automobiles.] I. Title. II. Series: Wheels (Minneapolis, Minn.)
    TL220.C68 1995
    629.25' 02--dc20   94-7084
                                                              CIP
                                                               AC

ISBN: 1-56065-211-X

99 98 97 96 95 94   8 7 6 5 4 3 2 1

Table of Contents

Michael Brown stands with the Aztec (foreground) and the Voltsrabbit. The Voltsrabbit was originally gasoline-fueled.

Chapter 1

What Is an Electric Car?

An electric car is a car that is powered by an electric engine. Instead of putting gasoline in the tank, you just charge the **battery**. These cars don't make smoke or burn up gasoline.

And they're becoming a very popular item. Just about every auto maker is working on an electric car today.

Ford and Chrysler have built electric versions of their **minivans**. Japanese auto makers are actively developing electric cars.

The BMW E1 of Germany is one of many electric cars being developed in Europe.

In Europe, Volkswagen, BMW, Audi, Fiat, and Peugeot all have electric cars on the way.

All kinds of businesses are starting electric car projects. The Swiss company that makes Swatch watches is planning an electric car. Vehma Corporation in Canada builds an electric version of a General Motors van. Independent auto shops are working on battery-powered automobiles, and mechanics are converting old cars to electric engines.

Electric cars are the future.

**The GM Impact
electric car**

Chapter 2

How Electric Cars Work

The electric car is quite different from a "standard" car that uses gasoline. From the outside it may look the same, but lift the hood and it's a whole new world.

The Engine

The engine creates the power that moves a vehicle. In a standard car, the engine power comes from a series of small, controlled explosions of gasoline. The power of each explosion pushes a piston, which pushes a rod, which turns a shaft. Eventually the power turns the wheels of the car.

Controlling the explosions and moving the power from the pistons to the wheels is a complex and dirty process. Many parts can break or wear out.

And gasoline engines need constant care. The oil must be changed, **spark plugs** replaced, belts checked, and more.

The engine in an electric vehicle uses electricity as its driving force. There is no burning gasoline and no smoke. Also, in most electric motors there is only one moving part. This means an electric car rarely breaks down or needs repairs.

And electric cars are quiet. There is no knocking engine or roaring **exhaust**.

The Battery

The electricity that powers the electric car's engine is stored in the battery.

An electric car battery is very much like the batteries you use in a flashlight or a video

The battery is a key component of all electric cars. Batteries come in all types, shapes, and sizes.

game. Like a sponge, a battery soaks up and stores electricity. When the charge in the electric car battery has been used up, you just recharge it. That means you plug it in to an

Chrysler TEVan
(Electric Minivan)

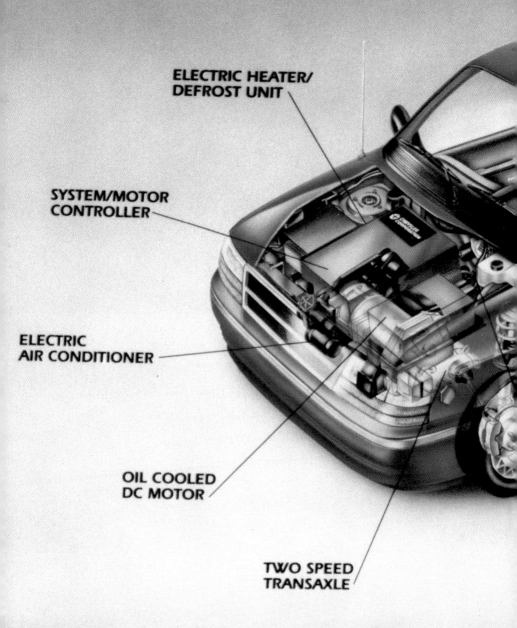

ELECTRIC HEATER/
DEFROST UNIT

SYSTEM/MOTOR
CONTROLLER

ELECTRIC
AIR CONDITIONER

OIL COOLED
DC MOTOR

TWO SPEED
TRANSAXLE

NICKLE/IRON
BATTERY TUBS

DRIVER SIDE
MINIVAN AIR BAG

ELECTRIC
POWER-
ASSISTED
STEERING

CHRYSLER
CORPORATI

Recharging an electric car is as easy as plugging it in. In the future, charging stations like this one might be commonplace.

electrical outlet and refill the battery with electricity.

Right now, the batteries used in electric vehicles can only hold enough electricity to run a car about 60 to 150 miles (95 to 240 kilometers). And it takes 6 to 8 hours to recharge the battery.

The most commonly used batteries are made of lead and acid. The batteries for electric cars are very expensive–as much as $10,000.

Scientists are working to make a cheaper battery that can hold more electricity and be recharged more quickly. Until they do, electric vehicles will only be useful for short trips.

The Body and Chassis

Some new electric cars have an entirely new body and chassis. The chassis is the skeleton or frame to which the other parts are connected.

Some new electric cars use ordinary car bodies, in which mechanics replace the old engine with an electric engine. Some older automobiles are being **recycled** as electric cars.

Wherever the body of an electric car comes from, it must be lightweight. The lighter a vehicle is, the farther and faster its electric motor can take it before the battery needs recharging.

Photo courtesy of Smithsonian Institute

Chapter 3

The First Electric Cars

Electricity played an important role in the early history of the automobile. In 1900, more than a third of the 4,200 automobiles sold in the United States ran on battery power. By 1912, there were 34,000 electric cars in the United States. They were sharing the road with vehicles running on gasoline, steam, and horse power.

Early electric vehicles were especially popular in cities, where their top speed of 20 to 30 miles (32 to 48 kilometers) per hour was all that was needed.

Early Makers of Electric Cars

At the turn of the century, companies were making electric cars in the United States as well as Europe.

The Pope Manufacturing Company, the largest bicycle maker in the U.S., had made about 500 electric cars by the end of 1898. The Riker

1899 Riker

Electric Motor Company of America made electric cars and trucks from 1896 to 1902.

In France, the Krieger Company in Paris produced an electric car in 1897 that could go 15 miles (24 kilometers) per hour. The Krieger could travel 50 miles (80 kilometers) on a single charge.

Three years later, the B.G.S. Company in France made an electric car in that could go almost 180 miles (290 kilometers) before recharging.

The Milburn Company of Toledo, Ohio, made more than 7,000 electric cars between 1914 and 1927. The Baker Electric Company (later Baker, Rauch & Lang) made electric cars in Cleveland, Ohio, from 1899 to 1928.

Improvements in gasoline-fueled engines, and changing tastes, made electric cars less popular after 1920.

The 1967 Ford Comuta electric car was never taken seriously as an alternative to gasoline-powered cars.

Chapter 4
The Electric Car Revival

In the 1960s, auto makers started to think about producing electric cars again. Gasoline engines polluted the environment, which was becoming an important issue. Gasoline was also becoming more expensive. Maybe that old idea of electric engines needed a second look.

General Motors
General Motors Corporation brought out two **demonstration vehicles**, the ElectroVair and the ElectroVan, in the 1960s. Both of these

vehicles had their problems. The batteries were large, heavy, and expensive. And they often had to be recharged. On top of this, neither vehicle could get up much speed.

Ford

The Ford Motor Company showed the Comuta, an experimental electric car, in 1967. It was a tiny car, only 80 inches (203 centimeters) long. It was less than half the length of a 1967 Ford Mustang. The Comuta never made it to production.

American Motors

The Amitron was introduced by the American Motors Corporation in the late 1960s. It had a cruising speed of 50 miles (80 kilometers) per hour and a maximum driving **range** of 150 miles (241 kilometers) per charge.

The Amitron had several interesting features. The air-filled seats were intended to save weight, and the instrument panel looked like the cockpit of a helicopter.

The General Motors Electro Van

Sebring-Vanguard

This small company made and sold almost 2,200 Citicars in 1974 and 1975. These two-person electric cars were about 8 feet (2.4 meters) long. They could go about 40 miles (64 kilometers) per hour and travel about 45 miles (73 kilometers) before recharging. Although they couldn't take long trips, some of them are still being driven as **commuter cars**.

The Exxon Valdez drifts in
a wash of spilled oil.

Chapter 5

Green Cars
and Green Fuels

Cars that cause little or no pollution are called green cars. This is because they are friendly to the green earth.

A gasoline engine doesn't burn up all of the gasoline it uses. Some of the gasoline turns to heat and power, but the rest turns into other chemicals. These come from the car's exhaust pipe. According to the Environmental Protection Agency, more than half of the cancer-causing pollution in the air comes from gasoline engines.

Greener Fuels

To reduce pollution, many fuels other than gasoline can be used to power automobiles. Methanol, ethanol, hydrogen, and **natural gas** all burn more cleanly. Some of these fuels can be made from corn or even water.

Auto makers can fit gasoline engines with devices that burn up more of the chemicals in gasoline. This also reduces the amount of pollution released into the air.

This car burns propane, or natural gas.

Heavy traffic is one of the greatest causes of air pollution. Electric cars could help to reduce the amount of smog in busy urban areas.

Zero Pollution

But changing the fuel or adding a pollution-controlling device does not end the pollution. A gasoline engine still pollutes, and many states are determined to clean up their dirty air. California, where several cities have severe air pollution, is looking at laws that will ban polluting engines.

Electric cars themselves produce no air pollutants. They get their power from batteries. The batteries are recharged with electricity supplied by electric plants. These plants do make some air pollution, but electric cars still come out better than gasoline-powered cars. When you take the power plants into account, electric cars still produce one-tenth of the pollutants of gasoline-powered cars.

As a bonus, electric cars would lower our need for oil. Moving oil around the world

Solar-powered recharging stations would provide electricity without producing air pollution.

A member of the U.S. Coast Guard rescues wildlife after the Exxon Valdez oil spill.

results in oil spills in many places every year. Electric-powered cars would reduce this kind of oil pollution.

Recycle and Reuse

Most parts of electric car batteries can be recycled and reused when they are worn out. Older cars that are converted into electric vehicles won't end up in junk yards. And new cars won't have to be built to replace them.

Cleaning up after the Exxon Valdez in the Gulf of Alaska

Above, engineers spend long hours solving design problems of the Impact. *Below*, the huge battery system is lifted into place.

Chapter 6

Solving the Problems of Electric Cars

Despite their good points, you don't see too many electric cars on the road. There are still disadvantages that need to be eliminated before they can replace the gasoline-powered car.

Lowering Costs

Right now electric cars are much more expensive than standard cars. But this will soon change.

As more and more electric cars are made and sold, their price will come down. Experts predict that by the year 2003, electric cars will cost about as much as a standard car does. General Motors claims that its Impact car will be affordable.

The Impact was released in March 1991. It is a two-person car that can go 120 miles (193 kilometers) on a single charge. It is light, powerful, and stylish, and will reach the market by the mid-1990s. It is the most promising electric car now in development.

The General Motors Impact

A recharging station model

Longer Trips

Electric cars can only go short distances before they have to recharge. The batteries don't hold enough power for a cross-country drive. The top range is 150 miles (241 kilometers), and most cars can go no more than 75 miles (121 kilometers) on a single charge.

Recharging a battery still takes a very long time. In the future, there will likely be many more electrical outlets for recharging cars.

Electric cars use a recharging "plug."

These will be available at gasoline stations, at convenience stores, at curbside stops, and in home garages.

Speeding Up

No electric car can go much more than 75 miles (121 kilometers) per hour. Lighter car bodies and more powerful batteries will give electric cars more speed.

Heating

Cold weather also poses a problem. In a standard car, a fan forces extra heat from the engine through the heater and **defroster** and inside the car. Electric cars do not create any extra heat. How will their drivers stay warm and keep the windows frost-free?

Car makers hope to solve this problem in the new models they are developing.

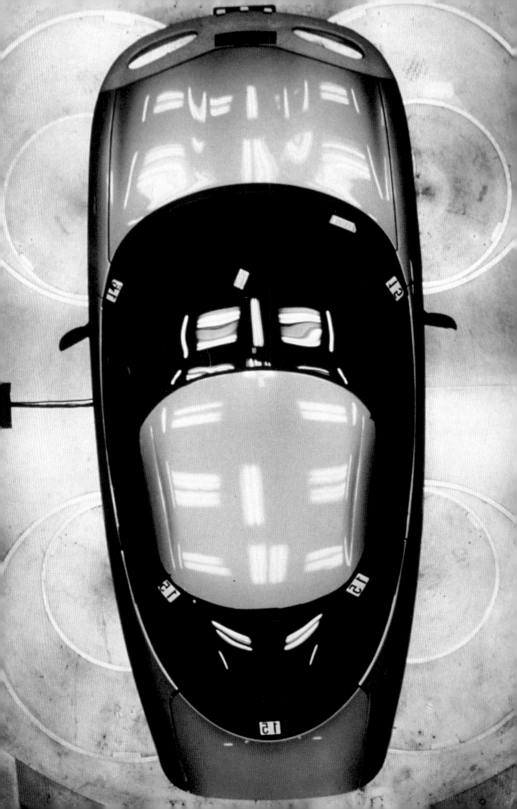

Chapter 7

The Future
of Electric Cars

In 1991 California passed a law that is
making electric cars more popular. The law
will require auto makers who want to sell cars
in the state to also offer some **zero-emission**
cars. That means the cars must release no
pollution into the air.

By 1998, according to this law, 2 out of
every 100 cars offered by an auto maker in
California must be zero-emission vehicles. By
2003, one of every ten cars must be zero-
emission. Auto makers have taken this law
very seriously.

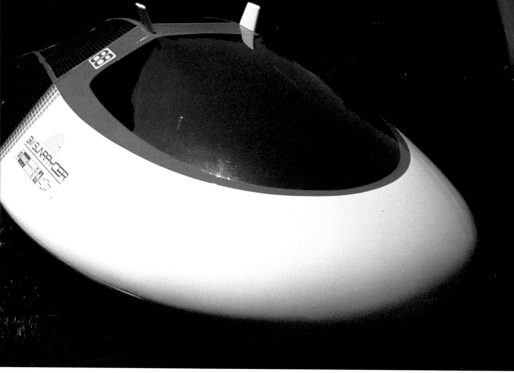

Modern electric cars are based on earlier experimental cars. The design of the Sunraycer (*above*), a solar-powered electric car, contributed to the GM Impact.

After all, California has more automobile buyers than any other state. If an auto maker wants to sell any cars at all in California, it must meet the goals set by this law.

Other States Follow

Nearly a dozen other states and the District of Columbia have followed California's lead. Among these are New York and Massachusetts, both very large markets for automobiles. By the year 2003, there should be nearly 300,000 zero-emission vehicles in the United States, even if no other states pass these laws.

Many other countries are considering laws that require the production and sale of zero-emission vehicles. Experts think that Japan, for example, will have 200,000 zero-emission vehicles on its streets by the year 2000.

The Impact will go through a lot of testing before its release to the general public.

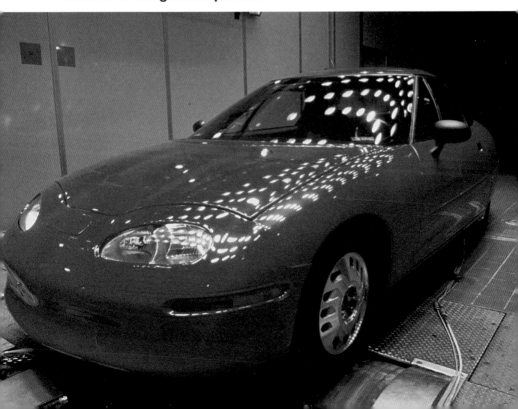

Glossary

battery–a device for storing and delivering electricity

charging station–a place for refilling a battery with electricity

commuter car–a vehicle used for short, daily trips to work or school

defroster–a heater that melts ice and frost from a car's window

demonstration vehicle–a car made to test and display a design and not meant for public sale.

exhaust–smoke and polluting chemicals created by a gasoline-powered engine

minivan–a small van for family use, with two rows of seats and storage room

natural gas–an underground gas that can be burned as a fuel

range–the distance an electric car can travel without being recharged

recycling–to save and reuse something

smog–air pollution caused by the exhaust from gasoline-powered vehicles

solar–powered by energy from the sun

spark plug–a device that ignites a mixture of fuel and air inside a gasoline-powered engine

zero-emission vehicle–a car that does not put chemicals or pollution into the atmosphere

To Learn More

Abels, Harriette S. *Future Travel*. Mankato, MN: Crestwood House, 1980.

Lincoln, John Ware. *Driving Without Gas*. Pownal, VT: Garden Way Publishing, 1980.

Lucas, Ted. *How to Convert to an Electric Car*. New York: Crown Publishers, 1980.

Willis, Terri and Wallace Black. *Cars: An Environmental Challenge*. Chicago, IL: Childrens Press, 1992.

Index

Photo Credits:

General Motors: cover, pp. 23, 32 (top and bottom),
34, 38, 40, 41; Shari Prange: p. 4; BMW: p. 6; Audi
of America, Inc.: pp. 11, 28; Chrysler Corporation,
p. 12-13; ETIC: pp. 14, 35, 36; The Smithsonian
Institute: pp. 16, 18; Ford Archives: p. 20; The U.S.
Coast Guard: pp. 24, 29, 30-31; Natural Propane Gas
Association p. 26; Greenpeace: p. 27.